THE TRUTH ABOUT

PTSd

Take a Look at Post Traumatic Stress from a Different
Perspective and Uncover the Disordered Truth About PTSd

CHAD M. ROBICHAUX & **JEREMY M. STALNECKER**
FOREWORD BY **ALLEN B. WEST,**
U.S. ARMY LT. COLONEL (RET.), U.S. CONGRESSMAN

My soul is in deep anguish.
How long, Lord, how long?
– Psalms 6:3

Endorsements

This book is a must read for all of us who have served, whether affected by PTS or not. If we haven't been, we likely know someone who has; and it's important for us to have perspective on what others are going through. It provides hope to those dealing with PTS and other post deployment adjustment issues because others like them have found a way to move forward.

Chad and Jeremy remind us that we are not defined by what has happened to us, or what we have done or not done. It gives perspective on what PTS is and how it affects us. In doing so it takes away excuses many of us use to not move forward with our lives. It challenges us warriors not to accept being a victim and to continue to fight for those important things in our lives worth fighting for (family, faith, community, country). And, it reminds us that we may not be the same as we were, but we can move forward and we can even grow.

– Colonel Doug Behseresht, USMC (Ret.),
Iraq & Afghanistan Veteran

I highly recommend this resource to anyone wanting to understand or help those struggling with Post Traumatic Stress (PTS). While not neglecting the medical research and explanations for PTS, Chad Robichaux and Jeremy Stalnecker share their personal stories, as well as draw from their experience of helping many warriors at Mighty Oaks. They examine PTS through the lens of God's creation and provide clear hope and direction in how to respond to PTS.

– Commander John Marc Wiemann,
US Navy (Ret.),
Lead Pastor of Cornerstone
Community Church of Atascadero,
Director of the Cornerstone Biblical
Counseling Training Center

A great resource for anyone struggling with PTS, loved ones of someone struggling with PTS, or anyone who has experienced significant trauma. Without minimizing the psychological impact of warfare on the soul, trauma is something we all experience if we live very long. As Chad and Jeremy so eloquently point out, trauma shouldn't be a destination or an obstacle to moving forward in life. Our pain might take us out of the fight temporarily but we can and must move on. In their book, Chad and Jeremy provide the tools and lay the foundation for moving beyond the pain and living the life God has called each one of us to live; "the abundant life" Christ promised. It's a foundational principle of Mighty Oaks. Our pain should never be an excuse for giving up. And, no matter what is taken from us in life, Chad and Jeremy make it clear that we can always choose to move forward!

– Lieutenant Colonel Rick Wolf,
USMC Reserve,
Director of Soul Survivor Outdoor,
A Military and Veteran Outdoor Adventure Company

To write this book "The Truth about PTSd", one must have lived it. Having served in Vietnam Nam, I can imagine the harsh memories that the writing process brought back, along with the haunting nightmares. The reality that Chad and Jeremy put into words is an honest representation of the devastating effects that PTSd can have on ones life. Despite their struggles they have given others a hope; a hope to overcome PTSd. In Chad's on words "do not let the past rob you of the future". The Truth about PTSd is a must read not only for the military. but also civilians and their families that have experienced trauma in their lives.

— **Thomas G Fordyce, USMC (Ret.)**
Vietnam Veteran and Purple Heart Recipient

Those who suffer from the stress and trauma of war want to heal. But there are many myths and misconceptions circulating about PTSd. "You are broken." "Try harder and get over it." "Just don't think about it." "Take this pill, you'll be fine." If a person tries to formulate a strategy based on erroneous intel, his or her objectives will never be realized.

Robichaux and Stalnecker have put together a clear, concise surgical strike against these faulty ideas, and given PTSd sufferers powerful tools and concepts that will aid them in their return to strength, stability and resiliency. Their insights are based on best practices from the medical and psychological communities, timeless principles from the Bible, and their own experiences as combat veterans. If you are a warrior who has been knocked down, this book will teach you how to get up again, written by warriors who have been there.

– Chris Adsit
National Director, Branches of Valor,
Author of The Combat Trauma Healing Manual

The words in this book, "You may have been hurt, but you have not been broken" is the theme throughout this book. It provides hope to those struggling with PTS and reminds them that they can fight through their struggles by being the warrior they are created to be. It helps turn Post Traumatic Stress into Post Traumatic Success.

— **Bruce Stewart**

Director of Stronger Alliance,
Pastor of "We are Stronger" Movie

THE TRUTH ABOUT PTSd

© 2017 All Rights Reserved

Chad M. Robichaux and Jeremy M. Stalnecker

Limit of Liability/Disclaimer of Warranty: While the publisher and authors have used their best efforts in preparing this book, they make no representations or warranties with respect to the accuracy and completeness of the contents of this book and specifically disclaim any implied warranties of merchantability or fitness for a particular purpose. No warranty may be created or extended by sales representatives or written sales materials. The advice and strategies contained herein may not be suitable for your situation. The author and publisher are not engaged in rendering professional, legal or medical services, and you should consult a professional where appropriate. The authors and publisher shall not be liable for any loss of profit, nor any personal or commercial damages, including but not limited to special, incidental, consequential, or other damages.

All Scriptures taken from the Holy Bible:
English Standard Version ESV, Crossway Bibles, 2007. Wheaton ILL

All rights reserved. No part of this book may be reproduced or transmitted in any form or by any means except as permitted under Section 107 or 108 of the 1976 United States Copyright Act and with written permission from the author. All materials are legal property of Chad M. Robichaux and Jeremy M. Stalnecker. Unauthorized duplication is strictly forbidden and punishable to the maximum extent under applicable law.

ISBN: 978-0-9863193-0-3
Edited by: Kate Lehman
Cover Design by: Barbie Ray Designs
Published by: *Making Life Better Publishing*
Learn more information about the authors at:
www.TheTruthAboutPTSdBook.com

THE
TRUTH ABOUT

Presented to:

_____

From:

_____

On This _____ Day of _____ , 20 _____

Table of Contents

Foreword

Lt. Col. Allen B. West, US Army (Ret.)
Member, 112th US Congress

My family is one based upon a simple premise, service to the Country. My Dad was a World War II Army veteran. My oldest Brother served in Vietnam as a combat infantry Marine. My Mother was a civilian servant to the 6th Marine Corps District Headquarters in Atlanta for nearly 25 years. My Nephew is currently serving as a Major in the US Army, an artillery officer, just as I was for 22 years. And our youngest daughter, Austen, is a college junior, contracted to become an Army officer.

My wife Angela is the daughter of a US Army combat infantryman who served two tours in Vietnam. He was laid to rest at his final duty station of Arlington National Cemetery. She has two Brothers who served in the US Air Force.

This is what has defined America for all of her 241 years of existence. It has been men and women who have been willing to step onto their own Lexington Green. Those who have stood upon freedom's ramparts, to serve and protect as Guardians, Watchmen on the wall of liberty. Standing their watch to ensure the principles and values we hold dear shall not perish from the earth.

They are the ones who answer the call to arms, rushing to the sound of the guns, willing to give that last full measure of devotion. Oft time we honor them with our words, accolades, medals, and ceremonies – or sometimes the kind gesture of picking up the tab for a meal or drink. However, throughout history, there has been an unseen enemy, a hidden adversary that has had a detrimental, and horrific effect, on our Warriors.

We who have been on the field of battle have called it by different names – combat stress, battle fatigue, and the thousand-yard stare. It represents the battle scar that we do not see, and many do not discuss. And I wear a simple black ring on my trigger finger of my salute hand to signify the current tragedy. It is called the #22Kill ring, and it reminds me, and others who ask me, that we have on average, per day, 22 of our brave combat veterans who are taking their lives. Imagine what we would say, what would be in the newspapers, if we had a combat engagement per day, where our troops were being killed at that rate? This is no different., Why are we not bringing this to the national attention?Most people can tell you more about Kim Kardashian or whatever pop culture topic is hot than the tragedy that is taking the lives of 22 veterans per day.

If in combat we were losing twenty-two troops per day there would be a media frenzy. Of course this would depend on who sits in the White House. Nevertheless, it would be a major story. Why not this? Is it that we lose focus when our men and women return home, other than the gracious random acts of kindness and gestures? Do we truly know what is ailing our Warriors? Do our Warriors truly open up to us and tell us they are hurting?

As a combat veteran, when I deployed a Battalion to Iraq in 2003, I tried to get my Soldiers to understand that the person they were here, had to stay here. There had to be a different person that boarded that plane, and set foot in a foreign land, called upon to do a mission for which our Nation had called us to complete. And when that mission was complete, that person over there, had to stay there. It is a tough thing to accomplish, compartmentalizing like that. Some would say that is not healthy, but we all must find a way to contend with that which is above and beyond what human nature consists, the struggle of combat.

Former Force Reconnaissance Marine Chad Robichaux has been there, and experienced the crucible of combat in the most personal manner. He is representative of that elite, cutting edge Warrior that this Nation has produced. Some would say that as warfare had developed from having to thrust a sword or a spear into the flesh of another in close combat things have changed. I would refute that assertion; it is still challenging to pull that trigger, regardless of the distance resulting in the loss of life of another. But the most primal concept of warfare has and always will be about individual, personal, survival. And on this current battlefield, especially against the global Islamic jihad, we find ourselves once again in close urban combat scenarios.

Chad was there, did it, got the t-shirts, and received the accolades for his service, his heroism. However, there were other wounds, scars, that he hid. And he hid those scars in the time-honored belief of "hey, I got this". Sadly, I have seen twice in my career, Soldiers who lost that battle and ended up taking their lives. Chad was almost there, but it was through a risen Savior, someone who dies for all of our sins, a living sacrifice . . . someone who said, "I got this for eternity" that enabled Chad to overcome, be the conqueror, a true Victor, not a victim. And so Chad started the Mighty Oaks Warrior Foundation to treat those wounds, the post-traumatic stress, that confronts our men and women when they leave the physical battlefield. Through this program Chad and Jeremy are saving lives, and this program is even being incorporated into basic training courses for our young Warriors transitioning into the Brotherhood of Arms.

Chad and Jeremy both know, there is only so much the physical world can do to heal an ailing spirit. Actually, there is nothing it can do. What is required is to trust in our Lord and Savior Jesus Christ. What is and always has been necessary is for that God shaped hole in all of us to be filled not with man's remedies, but the healing Spirit of the Lord.

Chad has shared with us his personal battle, and he wants to share his personal triumph. It is not just for those of us who have donned the uniform and served in combat. It is a guide, a lighthouse for us all, so that we will be the light that overcomes the darkness and the evil that is taking the lives of Americans. It is not just the PTS that our troops face, but it's also the opioid epidemic in this Nation. It is not a matter of more money being thrown at the issue. It is the recognition that such a scourge is not about the physical pain but the spiritual emptiness that can only be filled spiritually.

Combat warriors throughout history have put on armor to protect them on the battlefield. Chad and Jeremy bring to our attention the spiritual battlefield, and God's word, spoken through the Apostle Paul. Paul instructs us on how to prepare for the spiritual battlefield, a battlefield that is far more important.

Ephesians 6:10-18 (New International Version), *"Finally, be strong in the Lord and in his mighty power. Put on the full armor of God, so that you can take your stand against the devil's schemes. For our struggle is not against flesh and blood, but against the rulers, against the authorities, against the powers of this dark world and against the spiritual forces of evil in the heavenly realms. Therefore put on the full armor of God, so that when the day of evil comes, you may be able to stand your ground, and after you have done everything, to stand. Stand firm then, with the belt of truth buckled around your waist, with the breastplate of righteousness in place, and with your feet fitted with the readiness that comes from the gospel of peace. In addition to all this, take up the shield of faith, with which you can extinguish all the flaming arrows of the evil one. Take the helmet of salvation and the sword of the Spirit, which is the word of God. And pray in the Spirit on all occasions with all kinds of prayers and requests. With this in mind, be alert and always keep on praying for all the Lord's people."*

Be strong in the Lord, never give up hope, you're gonna do great things, I already know, God's got his Hand on you, don't live life in fear, forgive and forget, but don't forget why you're here, take your time and pray, thank God for each day, His love will find a way…these are the words I would say. – Sidewalk Prophets

– Lieutenant Colonel Allen B. West,
US Army (Ret.)

Member, 112th US Congress

Board of Directors, National Rifle Association

Preface

By Chad M. Robichaux
Force Reconnaissance Marine
& Afghanistan Veteran
President & Founder, Mighty Oaks Foundation

*There is a time for everything, and a season for
every activity under the heavens:
a time to be born and a time to die,
a time to plant and a time to uproot,
a time to kill and a time to heal,
a time to tear down and a time to build,
a time to weep and a time to laugh,
a time to mourn and a time to dance,
a time to scatter stones and a time to gather them,
a time to embrace and a time to refrain from
embracing,
a time to search and a time to give up,
a time to keep and a time to throw away,
a time to tear and a time to mend,
a time to be silent and a time to speak,*

a time to love and a time to hate,
a time for war and a time for peace.
– Ecclesiastes 3:1–8

Son to the warrior-king, David, and arguably one of the wisest men to ever live, Solomon wrote Ecclesiastes to share his wisdom gained through life's triumphs and trials. This was Solomon's message: In life, everything has its time.

Those of us who have been privileged with the opportunity to serve as military warriors in the cause of freedom, have faced experiences outside of life's norm, sometimes witnessing and participating in both horrific and heroic acts. In many cases, some of these events build us up and others nearly destroyed us; mentally, physically, and spiritually.

The struggles of my life started far before I became a Marine. I experienced a childhood of physical abuse from a Marine Corps Vietnam veteran father, the abandonment of my parents, and the great pain caused by the murder of my teenage brother when I was only fourteen. When I joined the Marines Corps at the ripe age of seventeen years old, it was a fresh start at life and a chance to begin a new journey, free from the hardships of my past. I eventually fulfilled my childhood dream of becoming a Force Recon Marine, and it was everything I hoped it would be. Yet, while my new life was not without new struggles, it was ten years before I set foot in a real-life combat zone.

The latter end of eight deployments as part of a special operations task force, began to catch up with me, and I found that the intensity and anger that had become my norm was being replaced by a state of anxiety and even moments of fear and hopelessness about the future. Initially, I was completely naïve to what the problem might be: an illness, a mental problem.... I was clueless, but I definitely knew something was wrong. When the physiological symptoms set in, I noticed my arms and the cheeks of my face would go numb, and I felt as if my throat were swelling shut. There were moments when I felt my heart was going to stop. I was fearful and ashamed to tell anyone on my team because I believed they would think I was weak and I knew I'd be pulled from my job. I shoved it way down and tried to push through it, but it only progressed. There were many times I thought I was having a heart attack. Other times, I felt out of body and started to have lapses in memory. Even though I'm not a drinker, I tried to drink whiskey on a few occasions to numb it. That only made it worse. I thought I was going insane.

It was during an operation when I was working alone with only local nationals that I realized how foggy my mind had become; I couldn't recall much of the prior two weeks. In a brief moment of clarity, I realized I had made decisions that put me in danger, and I finally had to speak up. A short time later I was back in the States sitting across from a clinical psychologist who told me I had been diagnosed with PTSd. That was devastating, and I felt in a single moment that I had lost everything. I had faced many physical injuries during my life, but I had always been able to work around them and continue. Yet, no physical injury had ever knocked me down like this atomic bomb that exploded in my soul. Never in a million years would I have thought that I'd suffer from such a diagnosis.

Due to my security clearances and the nature of the programs I was involved in, this diagnosis resulted in immediate removal from my job, teammates, and what I believed was my only purpose in life. I was not only devastated but also ashamed and lost. I felt I had failed—and in part I was told I had. I had put everything into our mission and my occupation as a warrior. I found myself lost and hopeless, feeling a mixture of shame, guilt, and overwhelming panic. I felt that if I honestly expressed my feelings, they would put me in a straitjacket and lock me in a padded room. The fear of being institutionalized for a mental deficiency was terrifying. I felt as if I were losing all sanity and would either crack or my body would stop functioning and I would die. Panic attacks became the new norm for me, and I became increasingly frustrated and angry at everything.

This state of mind was a self-fulfilling-prophecy that devastated the world around me and those who loved me, nearly costing me everything, including my family by divorce and my life by almost becoming another veteran suicide statistic. But I didn't want to end it all. I just needed to somehow escape my pain. The truth was I had realized the damage and pain I was causing to those I love and wanted to spare them of the misery I had brought them. I had somehow convinced myself that my family might be sad with me gone, but they would be much better off. This terrifying reality, unfortunately, finds a home in the hopeless hearts of twenty plus veterans per day, and nothing could be further from the truth.

However, through the intervention of my wife and others who love me, I was challenged to get up and get back in the fight. I was shown the way forward through the restoration of my faith, mentorship, and coming to the understanding that my future is not based on the past events in my life, but the choices I make moving forward.

And one of those choices I made was to not be bound by a clinical diagnosis that says I am somehow disordered and incapable of a future that is full of hope, joy and purpose. As warriors, we are not victims and should not relish the role of being broken, disordered or a dependent on a healthcare system. Some clinical programs for combat trauma are necessary, but these should be pit stops on the road to recovery, not a permanent destination.

Today, I stand on the other side of those circumstances. I know that the struggles I have overcome do not weaken me but have in fact molded me into the man I am today. I have learned great lessons, and I must share them with others who are facing or will face similar struggles so that we can endure them and emerge on the other side as the men and women God created us to be.

One of the most insightful and encouraging things I have discovered in my own path to healing is the perspective of seeing this PTSd thing through the lens of Creation. When I stopped looking at my mind and body's reaction as a problem, as a disorder, and understood it was normal for me to respond this way, everything changed for me. In fact, God Himself designed my mind to respond in such a way to trauma. I saw my situation differently and realized I wasn't disordered but was functioning perfectly—by design. You see, our brains and bodies are brilliantly designed to respond normally to the abnormal events of trauma to survive and protect us. That is not a disorder, but a blessing to embrace and be thankful for. Understanding this empowered me to move forward.

One of the great lessons I have learned from my own experience and experiences shared by other great military warriors is that we have a choice in how we respond to the experiences of our life. As we look back at our past, we must come to our own realization that however tragic (or heroic) those events may have been, they are not what led us to where we are today. Instead, it's our daily choices. When we can bring ourselves to that realization and take responsibility for our past and future, only then can we move forward into a future of restoration, hope and new purpose.

The information in this book was by no means written to deny the hardships that come after a traumatic event, the struggles of life, or even a "PTSd" diagnosis. In fact, I personally am all too familiar with the sleepless nights and overwhelming panic that is experienced when the physiological effects surface and you feel like you've lost control and all hope is gone. Trauma, PTS, and its symptoms are very real and it is a real problem, but there is also a solution and a path forward. The pages of this book are meant to disarm the thought that PTS is a life sentence, a disorder, and that a bright and purposeful future is lost due to a diagnosis. We were all meant for something more, something greater than the valleys of life. Yes, there is a time to war, hate, kill, tear down, weep, and to mourn, but there is also a time to love, to build, a time for peace and to laugh and dance again. There is a time to live again—with joy and purpose. Don't let your past rob you of your future. Get up, get back in the fight and make a choice to step into the freedom that is available for each of us who will not buy into a diagnosis that suggests we are disordered for a lifetime. You were made for something more!

Introduction

By Jeremy M. Stalnecker

USMC Infantry Officer & Iraq Veteran

Executive Director, Mighty Oaks Foundation

One of the greatest privileges of my life was serving with First Battalion, Fifth Marines during Operation Iraqi Freedom. Becoming a Marine and leading in combat were dreams that I had held since I was young. My grandfather served in Europe with the Army during the war and even though he did not talk much about it, I have always been thankful to have that as a part of my family heritage. My dad, although not a veteran, was outspoken in his support for those who were. My sisters and I were taught at a young age that military service is an honorable pursuit.

This is why, in many ways, going into Iraq as an infantry Marine was a dream come true. It was the culmination of a life's goal to honor those who served before me, defend the ideal of freedom for which my country stands, and go into battle with the very best warriors on the planet. The experience did not disappoint. I watched young men do things and overcome obstacles that those who weren't there would never believe. I was with these young men in the middle of the night as we waited to penetrate a berm that served as the dividing line between the relative safety of Kuwait and the great unknown of Iraq. These same warriors, undaunted by the enemy, fatigue and an unforgiving landscape pushed forward long after most would have stopped. I was with them when they attacked the heart of 2003's "most dangerous city in the world" and gave no thought to seizing the Presidential Palace once owned by the now infamous dictator Saddam Hussein. They did the impossible and did it with the honor and courage that has defined generations of America's war fighters. These were the best, and I had the honor of being included in their ranks.

Shortly after we came home, I left the

Marines and, as did many others, moved on with my life. I lost touch with most of the men that I had served with as work and family took their place. While the wars in Iraq and Afghanistan dragged on, I did my best to keep track of Fifth Marines and some of the guys that I knew who were still fighting but did a poor job of actually staying connected. Some of this was a lack of opportunity and some was willful ignorance. Every time I heard about an engagement that included Fifth Marines, I felt guilty, like a guy who had walked away from his family. I knew that I had done my time and was proud that I'd brought "my Marines" home safely, but I had to mentally and emotionally detach from the reality that some were still fighting in order to focus on the life I was now living.

As time went on, I started to hear about this thing called Post Traumatic Stress disorder (PTSd). When I returned from Iraq, I went through a period where I struggled to adjust and get my head around some of the things that I had experienced, but a strong support system, both before and after the military, allowed me to work through those challenging experiences relatively quickly. I still struggle with anger and other "leftover" issues from my time of service, but I believe that I am a fairly well-adjusted human being. So when I began to hear about those who were diagnosed with PTSd and its various symptoms, I had a hard time believing it was real. How could the men I had served with, the men who had the courage and fortitude to move into another country uninvited and kick out a homicidal dictator, struggle with the things that were being described? I could not get my brain around the fact that the warriors I had once known were now unable to function in their homes and communities. I knew that I had to work through some of my own issues, but certainly there was nothing wrong. I concluded that PTSd was for the non-warfighters and could not be as big an issue as everyone was saying.

Ten years after I left the Marines, I had the opportunity to meet up with a small group of guys from the old platoon. We were invited to a one week program put on by the Mighty Oaks Foundation for veterans dealing with combat trauma issues. At the time, I wasn't even sure I believed in combat trauma issues, but thought it would be a good opportunity to see some of my old Marines. They had done a better job of keeping up with each other and over the course of the week told me many of their stories. They were stories of suicide, broken homes and broken lives. I learned about warriors who now struggled to keep jobs. I also heard about business owners and entrepreneurs and those with great families and bright futures. Different people with the same experience that caused some to grow and some to struggle. While I still don't have it all figured out, that time with those men put me on a course that would lead to the job I have now with the Mighty Oaks Foundation. Two things became clear for me that week: My time of service did not end the day I put my uniform in the closet for the last time; and I needed to know more about Post Traumatic Stress disorder (PTSd).

This book was written to share with

you many of the truths those of us at Mighty Oaks have discovered about this "disorder" that is destroying families, stealing individual purpose, and causing many who have served to take their own lives. This is not intended to be a comprehensive study on PTSd and will in no way reflect the mountain of research that is being done to better understand this topic. It is intended to provide hope to individuals and families who have concluded that they are destined to live in a dark hole of despair without purpose or direction and to show that there is a path to overcoming this thing that has sidelined so many warriors who have given so much. While we do not write from a clinical perspective, we do write from the perspective of combat veterans who have both struggled with PTSd and helped thousands of others who have also struggled. There is hope and freedom on the other side of trauma, but not until you understand some essential truths that will make that freedom possible. It is our prayer that this book will help you to begin a journey no longer defined by your past but with a future full of hope and promise. Let's start the journey together as we consider The Truth about PTSd.

CHAPTER ONE ·

Moving Target

Imagine yourself sitting in a Forward Operating Base (FOB) in Iraq as enemy mortar rounds begin to fall. You immediately jump up and get the men in your team to shelter, but one of your guys is in no hurry. This type of attack has happened frequently, and so far, no one has been hurt but you would rather not take any chances. As you try to get him moving, one of those rounds comes through the roof and kills this team member as he is putting on his boots. That traumatic event will be forever stored in your memory and the next time you need to move quickly, your mind may tell your body that you are in the same danger as you were at the FOB.

Now you're at home, thousands of miles from combat, trying to get your daughter out the door for school. She's putting on her shoes, but you're going to be late and she isn't moving as fast as you think she could. Suddenly you feel physiologically like you did when your team member was killed. That absolute sense of urgency comes over you, and even though there is no danger, you explode on your daughter who is taking too long. You begin screaming at her like one of our guys in combat to move faster, and while you know you are out of control you don't stop. While your behavior toward your daughter is not okay, a historical event created an environment where it was natural for you to respond that way. As damaging as situations like this can be, the question that must be asked is, "How do I move forward without letting trauma control me?"

While there are many different thoughts on PTSd, what it is and is not, the truth is extremely complicated. We know that trauma can have real life consequences and that those consequences can be devastating both individually and collectively when a family has one or more members struggling to overcome trauma. Although the study of PTSd is a relatively modern area of psychology (it was first added as an actual psychological diagnosis in the third addition of the Diagnostic and Statistical Manual of Mental Disorders in 1980),[1] the impact of trauma has always had a name. What we know as PTSd today was called Nostalgia in the 1700's, Soldier's Heart and Railway Spine during the Civil War, and Shell Shock during the First World War. During the Second World War PTSd was better known as Battle Fatigue and would later be called Combat Stress Reaction before finally receiving the name Post Traumatic Stress disorder.[2]

Although the name has changed and the study of post-trauma behavior has gained more attention, the diagnosis of PTSd remains anything but a perfect science. The difficulty is that PTSd is not diagnosed by testing changes in physiology but by pairing up symptoms with a traumatic incident. The diagnosis is given when a person exhibits one or more behavioral symptoms and can articulate that those symptoms began after a traumatic life event. The symptoms generally fall into one of eight categories as directed in the Diagnostic and Statistical Manual of Mental Disorders, Fifth Edition (DSM-5[3]), and only one symptom from one event is needed to obtain a diagnosis.

Even though diagnosis is complicated, the basic mechanism that causes the post-trauma symptoms is more clearly understood, and helpful, in the right setting. In an article written for the Washington Academy of Sciences, Sethanne Howard and Mark Crandall describe the brain process that leads to many of the PTSd symptoms.[4] It is important for us to understand a little of their work on a very basic level before we move on.

If we think of the brain in the simplest terms, it consists of the frontal lobe where, among other things, logical thought takes place. When we observe a situation or activity and make a decision based on that observation, that process takes place in the frontal lobe. This process was defined by Air Force Colonel John Boyd as the OODA (Observe, Orient, Decide and Act) Loop and has been used in tactical instruction of soldiers, from pilots to infantry unit commanders, as a tool to disrupt and defeat the enemy.[5] The application outside of the military is obviously very important and equips us to move through our day making the thousands of decisions, large and small, that are needed for us to function in our world.

The second part of the brain is the limbic system, which makes up the inner border of the brain cortex. This is where subconscious thought takes place. As opposed to the OODA Loop process, the limbic system controls things that we instinctively do without going through a process of formal thought. This system controls the four "F's": fight, flight, feed, and fornicate—all primal and instinctive properties. This system:

- Stores historical data, allowing our brain to memorize proper responses to situations

we previously experienced, such as
trauma.

- Stores trained responses to specific
  situations that allow us to respond without
  conscious thought.
- Stores situation-specific responses created
  by a traumatic event.

When a traumatic event is experienced,
the limbic system immediately stores the event for
our future survival. This process is one of God's
fail-safes in our design. That traumatic event is
stored regardless of our conscious recollection
of it, and our body is prepared to respond to
protect itself based on anything that triggers that
response. Those triggers could be based on any
of our senses: smell, feel, touch, taste, or sight.
Whatever physiological effects we experienced
during the initial incident are stored as a default.
If triggered, our body immediately goes back to
the settings of that day: heart rate, adrenaline,
vision, audio exclusion, hyper-vigilance, etc..
Research on this dates back to the early part of

the last century, when scientists B.F. Skinner and Ivan Pavlov demonstrated that it is possible to condition involuntary responses using the appropriate stimuli.[6]

The physical changes that take place in the body and brain following trauma are beginning to be understood, but most treatments for these changes are still experimental. Generally, PTSd is treated as a mental or emotional disorder with medication and psychotherapy. The goal of this treatment is to make it possible for the sufferer to "get by." One of the interesting and complicated difficulties of PTSd is that no one treatment works for everyone. Each person, it seems, is a clean slate that doctors and therapists will throw various treatments at until something sticks. This can be one of the most frustrating aspects of PTSd for both the sufferer and those who care for them. While the science of this is still evolving, one thing we do know is that PTSd is very common. The National Center for PTSd provides some important statistics:[7]

- 70% of adults in the U.S. have experienced some type of traumatic event at least once in their lives.
- About 7 or 8 out of every 100 people (7-8% of the population) will have PTSd at some point in their lives.
- About 8 million adults have PTSd during a given year. This is only a small portion of those who have gone through a trauma.
- About 10 of every 100 women (10%) develop PTSd sometime in their lives compared with about 4 of every 100 men (4%).
- Women are nearly twice as likely to have PTSd as men at some point in their lives.
- The prevalence of PTSd among veterans of Iraq and Afghanistan is 13.8%.

One of the statements we make during the Mighty Oaks Program is that trauma is not a veteran issue; trauma is a life issue. While the data does indicate that combat veterans suffer from PTSd at a higher rate than the general population, it also makes clear that there are millions of people who have never seen combat but are struggling to get back on their feet after dealing with a traumatic life event. This is where I must be very clear: I am not drawing this distinction to say that combat-related PTSd is somehow insignificant or "common." I have seen first-hand the damage, both to individuals and families that combat related PTSd can and does cause. I only make the distinction to remind my fellow veterans that there are many individuals and families outside of the military community that need to understand how to move forward just as much as those who have served. This is a human issue that we would all do well to address so that anyone who endures trauma will be able to find hope and purpose on the other side.

As the study of both the physiological and biological impact of PTSd continues to develop, the expectation is that our understanding and treatment will as well. There are many good organizations and individuals working to bring clarity to an otherwise confusing issue.

The problem in all of this is that as we wait for a breakthrough in treatment, those who are struggling resign themselves to a life where the primary goal is making it from one day to the next. Since our knowledge of PTSd is constantly evolving, there is little hope for the person who has been diagnosed of ever getting "better." And so, instead of identifying the trauma as a serious life event and learning how to move beyond it, many will allow that event to define who they are. A moment in time, a traumatic and abnormal one to be sure, now becomes the lens through which every action, thought, and relationship is filtered, often with devastating effect.

And this is the problem. A medical community that is still working to get a firm grasp on how exactly to classify and deal with Post Traumatic Stress has declared that those who have it are broken. The word used is "disordered."[8] The implication: instead of PTSd being something that can be addressed and overcome, the sufferers are destined—because they are disordered—to struggle for the rest of their lives. Is it really a mystery, then, that the suicide, divorce and substance abuse rates among those who have been diagnosed is so high? When hope of moving beyond the trauma is removed, there is very little motivation to continue. It is as if the diagnosis is given and the one who has received it is locked in a cell with no expectation of ever being released.

This is, to me, what makes our view of trauma so important. Instead of simply accepting the label that is put on those who have dealt with a traumatic event and are living life as a slave to that label and that diagnosis, it important to understand the practical implications of PTSd and then develop a solid plan to move forward. Let's look first at the practical implication of PTSd.

CHAPTER TWO

Fight or Flight

PTSd carries with it some very real consequences. Any discussion of PTSd and combat trauma that tries to make coping nothing more than "try harder and get over it" can be extremely discouraging to the person who is struggling with trauma and its effects. Hope can be removed when we are unwilling to acknowledge that the brain and the systems that support it, as well as the individual emotional makeup of a person, can be profoundly impacted by traumatic events. Some of these things will never be fully repaired and the pre-trauma "normal" may not ever be the post-trauma "normal." In all of this, though, two things need to be understood.

First, it's OK to be different after experiencing trauma. Our fixation with getting back to a pre-trauma state or forgetting the traumatic event altogether is not practical or helpful. When medication is given to cause a patient to forget or to become numb to the memories, the emotional and psychological healing that can take place through normal processes has been stopped. This is the reason so many people will spend the rest of their lives treating the symptoms of their PTSd with medication. They have never given their bodies the time or opportunity to heal, and so they never will. This is probably a good time to take a quick aside and talk about medication.

Even though medication can numb a person to the point that healing cannot take place, at the right time and in the right quantity, medication is not necessarily bad. There are many who struggle so profoundly with anxiety and depression that they are not in a clear enough state of mind to make the decisions needed to get well. In these cases, the right dosage of medication can be helpful. It can be a tool used to get to the right place. Medication becomes harmful when it gets in the way of the body's natural healing process. In our Mighty Oaks programs, it is not uncommon to have students who are prescribed twenty or more daily medications! These medications are not intended to treat the problem, only to mask it. Our recommendation to anyone who sincerely seeks to get well is to actively work with his or her physician to understand what he or she is taking, why it's being taken, and the plan to get to the minimum dosage possible. While we would never advise someone to stop taking doctor-prescribed medication, there needs to be a plan in place to get to the point where it is no longer needed or at least needed at minimum levels. We need to focus on getting well instead of focusing on merely stopping or numbing the pain.

A traumatic event is not something that can be forgotten or simply moved past. It can, however, be a catalyst for growth as well as an opportunity to help others who are also struggling with trauma. Growth in any area of life often requires pain, but if we are willing to grow through the pain, we will become people we never could have been otherwise. The goal is not to get back to where we were before the trauma; the goal is to grow through it and become more fully equipped to fulfill our God-given purpose.

Second, we must understand PTSd, just as we do everything else, from the perspective of Creation. One of the interesting things about this discussion is that it is typically framed in the language of the victim. Even calling it a disorder implies that the one with the diagnosis is somehow broken. The person who has endured trauma is not broken—they're human! In our program working with the military and veterans, we never include the "D" in PTSd because we do not want to precipitate the idea that hardship in life is somehow uncommon. A disordered life is a life without trauma. And when we approach this topic and look for ways to move forward, we must grasp the truth that not only are we not broken when we deal with traumatic life events, but we are functioning exactly as our Creator, God, intended. If this is the case, then trauma, even severe trauma, does not have the ability to keep us from moving forward in our lives and relationships unless we allow it to. We are not broken. There is hope.

So, what does PTSd look like?

In the previous chapter we spoke briefly about the limbic system of the brain and how it works. There is of course much more to brain function than a book like this will allow us to cover, but even with the overview that was provided, we can see how the functions of this brain system are in place to protect us. As discussed, this system can store information one of three ways:

1. *It stores historical information so that we can respond to similar future situations in the right way.*

2. *It stores situation-specific responses.*

These first two are very similar and fall into the "fight or flight" category. This really is amazing when we understand that we were created with a mechanism designed to keep us safe. This is what allows us to learn, often without conscious thought, how to respond to dangerous situations so that when encountered at some point in the future, we will respond appropriately without thinking.

We have all experienced this to one extent or another. If you have reflexively pulled your hand away from an electric stove without thinking because at some point in the past you burned yourself, you have experienced this principle at work. You may not have known the first time you touched those electric stove coils that they were hot, but your brain recorded that information so that there would not be a next time. Consequently, even when the stove is off, your mind prevents you from putting your hand on it.

For those in combat, the principle is exactly the same. After observing a catastrophic event or suffering some degree of trauma personally, your brain stores everything that happened at the moment you were hurt or saw someone else get hurt and automatically responds when one of those elements is present again. It may be a sound or smell or the shape of a house—anything can cause your mind and body to respond as if the threat were right in front of you once again.

This is why someone who has experienced trauma will have many of the same physiological responses to a "trigger" even though they are not in danger. The body, in conjunction with the brain, is working to mitigate danger. What we call instinct or a "gut feeling" that we use to tell us when things just aren't right is often the limbic system alerting us of danger based on something that has happened in the past. An incredible mechanism that can keep us out of danger we may not even know exists.

3. *It stores trained responses.*

This third category is equally as amazing

and familiar to anyone who has done multiple repetitions of anything so that he or she could eventually do them without thinking. A quote often attributed to Martial Artist Bruce Lee is, "You need to train it until you forget it." This is the premise of running football plays until you can't get them wrong or drilling Jiu Jitsu moves until they become second nature. The limbic system is being trained so that these movements that take place in fractions of a second can happen with precision and speed, without the obstacle of conscious thought.

This process is especially familiar to anyone who has been through U.S. Marine Corps Boot Camp. Until I learned about this process of unconscious thought, I believed, as I am sure many Marines do, the constant yelling and moving as quickly as possible at all times while going through basic training was nothing more than a form of harassment. The Drill Instructors were harassed by other Drill Instructors who had been harassed themselves, and this process had probably been taking place since 1775.It was now our turn. I thought that it was to make the recruit hard or to somehow weed out the bad. In reality, contrary to the opinion of any recruit getting off the bus at Marine Corps Recruit Depot, the entire process is designed to train the limbic system, so that when that recruit becomes a Marine responsible for his own life and the lives of others in combat, he will move and respond instinctively. When every second may be the difference between life and death, the trained responses in the limbic system carry that Marine forward without being slowed down by having to observe, orient, decide, act.

This is the same process that police officers go through. They fire thousands of rounds through their service weapon, pulling it from the holster and replacing it each time, so that in the confusion and chaos of an armed conflict, they can instinctively draw their weapon and effectively employ it as necessary. It is extremely rare to hear of a police officer accidentally hitting an unarmed bystander or drawing the wrong weapon on their belt. They train to the point that they no longer need to think to do their job. The fact that we can learn subconscious responses to thousands of situations is strong evidence for a Creator who knew what He was doing!

Of course, just as we can step back and marvel at the design intended to keep us from harm, we must also acknowledge that the same responses at the wrong time or without the right context can be harmful and in many cases devastating. This does not mean that we are broken or that our design failed; it just requires that we understand what can happen as well as the harmful thoughts and behaviors that can potentially overwhelm us if we are not diligent. When are these responses bad?

1. Many of the responses associated with PTS and combat trauma can be personally and relationally damaging if they happen when you are not in danger. People who have been diagnosed with PTS are often described as "angry" or "having a short fuse." It is interesting because what can be

helpful in one scenario is just obnoxious in another. The story used to illustrate this at the beginning of chapter one can play out a thousand different ways in the various relationships in your life, and you must learn how to either respond correctly, not respond at all, or excuse yourself from the situation so that you won't respond inappropriately.

2. We have already stated that once you've experienced trauma, it is very unlikely that you will forget that event and may even remember it with most of the details intact. This is fine if you grow through the trauma and allow the memory of what happened to equip you to better serve others and more fully do what you were created to do. Some people, though, allow the memory of what happened to absolutely enslave them to a specific moment in time. They will not move forward because the memory of the past

occupies every unguarded moment. They need to diligently and deliberately fill those moments with positive thoughts and actions instead of allowing an event to define their lives. Many will never find freedom from those memories.

3. If there is one thing that we consistently deal with on the PTS side of our Mighty Oaks Programs, it is bad behavior. For some, trauma and difficulty are an excuse to behave poorly. There is never a good excuse to make a decision you know is harmful, but many think because they were hurt, abusing drugs and alcohol, chasing illicit relationships, and generally being a jerk are acceptable. They blame a PTSd diagnosis for their problems when really it is the bad decisions that they made following the trauma that have caused the majority of their difficulties. Bad behavior, with or without trauma, will always lead to destruction.

4. As odd as it sounds, there are many who have found an identity in their PTSd diagnosis and are unwilling to heal because they don't want to lose that identity. This is much more common in the veteran community than in others, but often those who have been diagnosed with PTSd wear that diagnosis as a badge of honor or as proof that they did something important and got hurt. I have a hard time understanding this and have found it to be extremely damaging to any attempt to get better. Outside of the veteran world, those who suffer trauma do their best to find some sense of normalcy as quickly as possible, but many times veterans act like the kid with the broken arm who wants to leave his cast on because of the attention it gets him. This is by no means everyone, but those to whom it applies will have a difficult time finding a larger sense of purpose.

5. While this next group is probably smaller than the others, there are those who hold on to their PTSd diagnosis because of the benefits that come along with it. We have almost incentivized those struggling with trauma by putting them in a situation where they are getting paid for their diagnosis and will lose the pay if they get better. While I believe everyone who served is entitled to whatever they are promised, mental and relational well-being should never be replaced by a paycheck. Some will, unfortunately, decide that a monthly check is more important than figuring out how to move forward.

6. Another harmful response to PTSd is the persistent belief among many who have been diagnosed that any counselor who is not also a combat veteran cannot possibly offer any helpful advice—unless someone has been hurt the way that I have been

hurt, they have no right to tell me what I should do. Interestingly, however, we don't carry this thinking over to any other area of our lives. We do not believe that a doctor needs to have had cancer to know how to treat it. We trust that he has studied and helped other patients with cancer and so, even if he has not suffered from it himself, he can prescribe the right course of treatment. While not all counselors have personally dealt with PTSd, many of them have spent years both studying and helping hundreds of individuals who have. The "you don't know what I have been through" excuse becomes a wall behind which many hide so that they are not held accountable for their behavior. This thinking takes away much of the helpful insight and advice that is available when counseling is approached with an open mind.

7. This last group has learned how to get everyone in their world—spouse, kids, and friends—to cater to their needs because of what happened to them. There is little motivation to get well because they have created an environment that has selfishly turned everyone else into their caregiver. Only you can know if you need a caregiver, but never be content to stunt your own growth and healing because those around you are willing to take care of you.

It's All About Perspective

God has built within us an incredible mechanism to provide safety and a high level of proficiency as we do the things that He has designed us to do. He does not intend to hurt us; rather, He equips us to be the very best that we can be, to have the freedom to accomplish everything that He sets in front of us. When we allow the events of our lives to dictate how we think, act and live, we have given that freedom away. Many will say that the freedom to grow, produce, and live a life of meaning was taken from them. They accept that they are disordered and embrace all that goes along with that brokenness. The only thing disordered is a definition of PTS that says we are. There are memories, feelings and emotional struggles that may never go away. However, we must understand that we never lose the power to choose how to respond to them.

CHAPTER THREE

Not Disordered

As difficult as life can be, it is not difficulty, or the trials, or even those moments when we feel so overwhelmed that we can't see a way forward that defeat us. The thing that defeats us, that makes us throw in the towel and decide that we don't want to go on, is a loss of hope. When we begin to believe that "this is just the way it is, and nothing will ever change," we condemn ourselves to a lifetime of drifting without purpose or direction on the sea of life. It becomes difficult to accomplish anything or fulfill the purpose for which we were created because we have accepted defeat as a way of life. We have accepted the label of "disordered" and resigned ourselves to just getting by. But it doesn't have to be this way. While we cannot control what happens to us, we can absolutely control our responses. Don't allow your circumstances or the decisions of others to define you or determine where you will end up. Much can be taken from you, but you never lose the ability to decide.

I have always been a student of history and have always found it fascinating that, throughout history, some have overcome incredible odds while others have not. There are many examples, of course, but perhaps none as poignant as the Jewish Holocaust during the Second World War. During the period from 1939-1945, it is estimated that more than six million Jews were killed at the hands of the Nazi army. Many of these were killed in the concentration camps spread throughout Europe to imprison and eventually exterminate European Jews. One of the incredible outcomes of this tragedy are the stories of men, women and children who refused to give in to the overwhelming trauma all around them. If anyone had the right to give up, it was the Jews, and yet, many of their stories illustrate the heroism that can be seen when people refuse to quit. One lesson we learn from these stories is that traumatic events are events outside of the normal course of life.

It is possible to respond to abnormal events in a perfectly reasonable way without surrendering to the hopelessness that overwhelms so many. This will seem abnormal to most people. But it is not only normal, it should be expected. In his book *Man's Search for Meaning* (which has sold more than 10 million copies), Holocaust survivor Viktor Frankl made this statement about these "abnormal" situations: "An abnormal reaction to an abnormal situation is normal behavior.[9]" He went on to explain that to *not* struggle with serious life trauma would be abnormal. This phrase has been simplified and can be found throughout the literature dealing with this topic. Even the Department of Veteran Affairs National Center for PTSd starts their discussion on this topic with the statement: "Normal

Reactions to Abnormal Situations." None of this is to say that there are not serious difficulties associated with trauma, only that the sufferer is not broken. The trauma itself is the problem, not our natural response to it.

This insight can be liberating to the person struggling with trauma if they will really get a hold of the truth found in what Frankl said. A Jew living in a concentration camp should struggle with the trauma that they have been forced to endure. To struggle is the normal response. It is the situation that is abnormal, not their response. Rape victims should struggle with the violence forced upon them. The trauma that they had to endure was extremely abnormal, and it would be strange not to have a difficult time. The warrior who has both taken life and seen those that he cares about lose theirs should experience grief and loss. The taking of life is abnormal, but processing grief is not. It is normal to respond to abnormal situations in a purely human way. In fact, to use behavior or substance to prevent the response to that abnormal behavior is, in itself, abnormal. We were created to respond to these situations in a way that allows us to process the events and all that accompanies them. It's normal.

As Frankl reflected on his time in concentration camps, he described the moment that he realized the key to his survival in the camps and happiness in life. Even though his captors could take almost everything away from him, the one thing they could not take was his ability to decide. "Everything can be taken from a man but one thing:" he said, "the last of the human freedoms—to choose one's attitude in any given set of circumstances, to choose one's own way.[10]" He understood that his life was not defined by what happened to him or where the circumstances outside of his control may have led. His life was defined by the decision he made every day, even in captivity, to be the very best person that he could possibly be. When talking about how people often say that their responses to trauma are out of their control, he said simply: "Between stimulus and response there is a space. In that space is our power to choose our response. In our response lies our growth and our freedom.[11]"

So much of the struggle with PTS comes from accepting that label of "broken" and failing to exercise our right to choose how we will respond to the events in our lives. When we finally decide that we are going to move forward in spite of trauma, we have taken the first step toward growing into a person who can leverage his or her pain for the good of others.

Once that decision has been made, what are some actions you can take to help continue walking that path?

1. Realize it is good to talk about what you have been through and seek out those who will understand. This is not bad-mouthing or talking about how hard you have it. This is processing the events as they happened and working to understand the lessons, both personally and for the good of others. Don't be afraid to share your own failings and shortcomings of how

you have dealt with things so far. They are all part of the story and only when we are honest with ourselves and others can true healing begin. When we refuse to talk with others about what has happened in our lives, we tend to have thoughts that are either not true or not healthy. The Psalmist said it this way in Psalm 32:3: "When I kept silence, my bones wasted away through my groaning all the day long." Telling your story, either to a group or to another person, gives you the opportunity to organize your thoughts and bring to light those that are harmful. Most people who have experienced trauma and then told their story to others will attest to the healing that comes each time the story is told. You must be careful not to get caught in a never-ending cycle of telling the same story again and again, but tell it and process it until it can be redeemed in your own life. Find some people that care for you and will listen without judgment and you will have the freedom to finally reveal what is going on inside.

2. Refuse to allow the past to define you. This is a decision that you will have to make every day at first and then less frequently as time goes by. The problem with trauma is that there is a voice inside your head that will tell you, as often as you are willing to listen, that you are no more than the sum total of that event. The voice says you should be embarrassed or angry or depressed because of something that happened in your past. The funny thing about that voice is that it gets louder the more you listen and quieter the more you stand up to it. Refuse to allow your past or the voices, real or imagined, in your life define you based on a particular event.

3. Replace your bad behaviors with good ones. As we discussed earlier, some

behaviors can be helpful in the right setting but absolutely destructive in the wrong one. Learn what these behaviors are and begin to intentionally replace them with other ones. Find something you can do that will occupy both your mind and body, so when you feel tempted by something that will hurt you or others, you can make yourself too busy to get in trouble. Be intentional so that you don't find yourself heading in a direction you would rather not go.

4. Regain purpose and direction by leveraging your story and gifts for the good of others. There is nothing more damaging than a lack of purpose and direction. God created each of us with a purpose, and gave us both the gifts and opportunities to fulfill that purpose. The fact to remember about God-given gifts is they are never given for self-glorification. They are given so we can glorify Him by

serving others. Use what He has given you to serve those in your life.

5.   Restore the relationships that have been lost in the wake of the trauma. Unfortunately, when trauma enters a life, some people we care about become collateral damage. Don't walk away from those damaged relationships if there is anything that you can do to bring restoration and healing. Remember, the healing you are working for is not just for you but for those in your life who also need direction. Restore the broken relationships and move forward with those who were close enough to you to get hurt.

How you handle trauma is up to you. You can allow it to define you and become the sum total of your life, or you can grow through it and become a stronger, more productive person than you were before the trauma. The choice is yours.

CHAPTER FOUR

A Walk Through The Valley

Those who have served in the military share a connection regardless of age, rank or branch. My favorite jokes to tell are any that make fun of a branch of service other than the Marine Corps, but even I take it personally when those who have not served make jokes about other branches. It's okay for us to make fun of each other, but not acceptable for others to poke fun at us. There is, it seems, a thread that ties all of those who have served or are serving to every other warrior who has picked up a weapon in defense of his nation and fellow warriors. Though the weapons and tactics may change, the heart that moves courageously forward in the face of imminent danger does not. We are all, regardless of age or generation, basically the same.

I believe this is why modern-day warriors find such a connection with many of the warriors described to us in the Bible. Regardless of a person's choice of theology, it is hard for someone who has experienced the hazards of war not to respect men and women who were not afraid to do what warriors do. The Bible tells stories of men who led armies and men who fought hand-to-hand with improvised weapons. We are told of a woman who led her nation to war and another who killed an enemy general by driving a tent stake through his head. The Bible is full of war-fighters whom we can respect and relate to, and in some way, even connect with through our own service. One of the best-known warriors in the Bible, though, is a man by the name of David.

David was a warrior's warrior. He first comes on the scene in one of the most well-known stories of the Bible by killing a nine-foot-tall giant by the name of Goliath. He was only a teenager but quickly became the hero of the nation of Israel. He would go to fight many battles and kill many enemies and is still revered today in modern Israel as a soldier and king.

But David was not without his problems. Even though we are told in scripture that he had a heart to please God, but because he was a fallible man David did things that violated the very laws of God and that he had lived to protect. Anytime we live outside of God's express will for our lives there will be consequences, and King David was no exception. This warrior King, who became the champion of his nation, struggled late in his life with rebellion from within his kingdom, a takeover of his throne and an attempt on his life. All terribly difficult trials, but, as if to add insult to injury, each were perpetrated by his own son Absalom (2 Samuel 13-19). David had the kind of life that many can relate to: The highs and lows of a soldier, overwhelming family issues, and a nurse to take care of him as his life came to a close because he could no longer take care of himself. This once great warrior had, at least from an outsider's perspective, lost everything that once made him great.

Curiously, David was not only a warrior, but also a writer and musician. He wrote many of the songs we find in our Bible under the heading of "The Psalms." These Psalms, or songs, were written to share the ups and downs of life in a way that could be set to music and easily understood. One Psalm has become perhaps the best-known scripture in all of the Bible. The 23rd Psalm is read at many funerals and special events where encouragement or hope are needed. While we do not know exactly when this Psalm was written, we know it was sometime late in David's life. Some have concluded that he wrote this as his kingdom was being taken from him by his son Absalom. Understanding that David did not write this after a major victory but rather in the midst of personal trials after a lifetime of combat, makes it that much more meaningful for those struggling with their own life trauma. If you are not familiar with this Psalm, I encourage you to think about the words as you read them:

> Psalm 23
> 1. The Lord is my shepherd; I shall not want. 2. He makes me to lie down in green pastures: He leads me beside still waters.
> 3. He restores my soul: He leads me in the paths of righteousness for His name's sake.
> 4. Even though I walk through the valley of the shadow of death, I will fear no evil: for You are with me; Your rod and Your staff they comfort me. 5. You prepare a table before me in the presence of my enemies: You anoint my head with oil; my cup overflows. 6. Surely goodness and mercy shall follow me all the days of my life: and I will dwell in the house of the Lord forever.

What do these verses say to you? One of the walls we like to build up around ourselves is the wall of "no one knows what it's like to be me." We typically say that as an excuse for our own bad behavior and justification for feeling sorry for ourselves. Realizing the author of these verses had a life filled with struggle and betrayal should bring down that wall and cause us to take a hard look at why he could write about peace and contentment in spite of his circumstances. David understood something that we would all do well to get a hold of: in life, we do not need to be defined, or enslaved, by our circumstances. David knew life was bigger than just him, and even when he did not *feel* like it, he *knew* he had a God who loved him and had a plan for his life. Even when circumstances seemed absolutely out of control, even when he may have wanted to step back and ask why, he could take comfort in the fact that the Great Shepherd, God, had never left him. He acknowledges in verse three that he was broken, but declares that even in his brokenness, he would find restoration! What powerful words when we feel broken and alone. There is hope, and as defeated as we may feel right now, the Good Shepherd will restore us if we will trust and follow Him.

As David wrote this, he was not naive to the difficulties that were still waiting for him. This realization is so difficult to deal with when we are trying to recover from trauma. It seems that just as we are beginning to make progress, we get knocked down with another trial. We get one area figured out and then start to struggle with our family, or at work, or with a health issue. It's as if we are constantly living between sets of waves just trying to get a breath before another wave crashes on top of us. It is imperative to remember that as long as we are living, we *will* struggle. Not because of trauma, but because living is hard! But that difficulty does not mean that God has abandoned us or stepped back to let us figure it out on our own. As we read these verses, we see that David stops talking *about* God and starts talking *to* Him. Look at verses four and five: He says that when he is going through the valley of the shadow of death, he will not be afraid. Why? Because "You (God) are with me!"

I don't know what the valley of the

shadow of death looks like in your life, but for David, I can only imagine that he was overwhelmed by how his life was turning out. For you it may be a loss of identity, broken relationships, or an overwhelming depression that takes you to places in your mind you never thought you would go. This walk through the valley is a walk that everyone will take, but a walk that ends in death only if we stop moving forward. This is not called "the valley of death" but "the valley of the shadow of death!" Death is just a shadow intended to scare us into complacency and despair. If we understand in those shadow of death times that we are not alone and trust the Shepherd who has always taken care of us, we will emerge on the other side of the valley.

I'm glad that David did not stop writing in the valley. He talks about protection and comfort and provision and a relationship with the Shepherd that will last forever! It can be extremely difficult to accept that God is with us and has a plan for our lives when it feels like everything around us is falling apart. But we can trust the words of another warrior, a guy who struggled just like the rest of us, that it will get better as long as we don't stop under the shadow. We will all find ourselves in the valley; following the Shepherd out of it into those greener pastures of life is entirely up to you.

Time To Move Forward

Some might ask why they see elderly war veterans who have only served in the military for a few years wear hats and jackets and belong to organizations that reflected their service. Many of them spent a couple of years in the military and then fifty plus years building a family and a business and rebuilding a country, and yet the accomplishment for which they are most proud is those few years of service. While that may seem strange to some, it shouldn't. For many, military service becomes the lens through which the rest of life is viewed. It colors every relationship and activity and provides a unique context through which most decisions are made. It becomes the center point of life around which everything else revolves. It is a moment in time that says, "I did something that most of the world has never done and in the process helped to write history." It may not be the most important season that has ever happened in life, but it becomes the standard against which everything else is measured.

And this is why it so difficult to accept the notion that Post Traumatic Stress is a disorder that will destroy the warrior when the enemies' bullets could not. We cannot accept that the warriors with whom we served, and many like them, have now lost the ability to get up and fight. We must not accept that. As challenging as our struggles may be, it's difficult to believe that those who once made the decision to step into a lineage of warriors that goes back to the ancient civilizations of the world, have decided that laying on the ground and letting people step over them is more acceptable than standing up and making a difference in their homes and communities.

This topic elicits strong opposing

opinions. Some in the veteran and military community disagree with the assertion that a decision can be made to have a productive life beyond trauma. There are some, in and out of the veteran community, who will not allow themselves to move beyond the title of "disordered," thus finding their identity in what has happened to them. It is also true that the very real issues presented by Post Traumatic Stress may never go away and are, in many cases, life-long struggles. Our purpose in writing this is not to downplay PTS or those dealing with it or to argue with those we simply don't understand. Our purpose is simple: We want to provide hope to those who have been told they are broken because of some past event they have had to endure. While people and events can steal moments from your life, they do not have the power to steal your future—*unless you give it to them.*

- You may have been hurt, but you have not been broken.
- You may have to deal with your past, but you do not have to let it define your

future.

- You do not have to be a prisoner to broken relationships, substance abuse or self-destructive thoughts.
- Regardless of how you feel, you can build a life that is meaningful.
- You can set the example for others to follow.
- You can be a positive influence in your home, your community, and your world.

We all get knocked down. Some harder than others. It is often traumatic and has life-long consequences. But getting knocked down does not mean that you must stay down. Your world needs the warrior who once sat in the dark waiting to engage an unknown enemy. Your community needs the warrior who once did what less than one half of one percent of their countrymen has ever done. Your family needs the warrior who once refused to let fatigue, hardship and an unforgiving environment keep them from fighting their way to the top. You need to be that warrior again and find the hope and purpose that once drove you to do the seemingly impossible. Instead of cursing the world as it passes you by, get up off the ground and use the days ahead to build a life of significance. You are not broken. You are not disordered. It's time to move forward.

APPENDIX

A Relationship with the Creator

"Therefore, if anyone is in Christ, he is a new creation. The old has passed away; behold, the new has come."
– II Corinthians 5:17

As we close this book it is important to take a few more pages and talk about how to have a relationship with the Creator. Our purpose for writing was to provide some insight into Post Traumatic Stress while offering hope in the process. However, we also know that true hope and healing comes when we align our lives with the One who made us. Only when we are living in fellowship with Him can we be fully what He intended us to be. We will never be able to move from finding our identity in what has happened to us to finding our identity in the One who loves us until we first put our lives in His hands.

Many of you already have a relationship with God through His Son, Jesus Christ. You have experienced the forgiveness of sins and the new life found when we surrender to the will of our Creator. It is an amazing thing to know that the One who created the universe and all that it contains desires to have a personal relationship with each one of us. As followers of Christ we are far from perfect, but we recognize our imperfection and rest in the One who gives us life. To be fully what we were created to isn't possible without this personal relationship. If you have accepted God's gift of salvation, you have all that you need to apply these principles of leadership and be the leader you were created to be.

Maybe you have not yet entered into that personal relationship. For one reason or another, you have not accepted that you can, and should, align yourself with God's eternal purpose for you. There are many reasons that people do not accept this gift. If you are reading this, you are clearly not averse to the Christian worldview. Perhaps you've been hurt or disillusioned by the behavior of those who call themselves Christians or are simply, and honestly, trying to make the best decision. Whatever the case, I cannot end this book without telling you how to have that relationship.

Having a relationship with God is about so much more than overcoming PTSd. But without that relationship, you can never truly be all that you were created to be and experience the healing and hope that comes when we have a relationship with our Creator. God created us to be perfect. There was no brokenness in the beginning, and we were in complete communion with Him. We are even told in the third chapter of Genesis that God would personally spend time each evening with the first humans.

But then mankind, through our common father Adam, decided to rebel against God's will and do what He had expressly told them not to do. This disobedience (what we call sin) broke our perfect relationship with God and made it impossible for man to walk in communion with Him. Because of sin, this broken relationship carries with it a penalty—separation from God forever in a place called Hell. Certainly not something we like to talk about, but a reality that we must all face.

The great light in this dark story is that God still wants to have a relationship with us and has made that possible through His Son, Jesus Christ. By accepting His gift of forgiveness of sins, each of us can be forgiven and given a new life through Him. Our relationship and communion with the Creator will be restored and our life will be in line with His purpose.

Having a relationship with Christ and

experiencing forgiveness of sins is not some formulaic process, but rather an acceptance of a gift freely offered to us by Him. Some thoughts for those who would like to enter in to that relationship:

1. *Recognize your condition.*
   To find the way to eternal life with God, you must admit that you are lost in sin. Romans 5:12 teaches us that since Adam and Eve, the first man and woman on earth, a sin nature has been present in all people. Romans 3:23 says, "For all have sinned, and fall short of the glory of God." Sin is any act contrary to God's laws and commandments, and the sins we have committed separate us from God. Sin has a penalty. Romans 6:23 says, "For the wages of sin is death; but the free gift of God is eternal life in Christ Jesus our Lord." The wage or payment for our sin is spiritual death and eternal separation from God.

2. *Realize that religion and good works are not the answer.*

    Religions try to create their own ways to God. Their systems may seem logical, but they cannot bridge the gap created by our sin. Proverbs 14:12 says, "There is a way that seems right to a man, but its end is the way to death." In other words, our thoughts and ways are not what matter. God's Word, the Bible, provides true answers of grace and forgiveness. In Ephesians 2:8–9 the Bible says, "For by grace you have been saved through faith. And this is not your own doing; it is the gift of God, not a result of works, so that no one may boast."

3. *The good news is that Jesus has made a way!*

    Even though we were lost and separated from God, He loved us. Because of that love, God sent His Son to die on the cross and raised him from the dead three days later. John 3:16 explains, "For God so loved the world, that he gave his only Son, that whoever believes in him should not perish, but have eternal life." Through the death and resurrection of Jesus, He became the payment for our sin. Now we do not have to pay for our sin ourselves. By His grace, salvation is provided. Romans 5:8 says, "But God shows his love for us in that while we were still sinners, Christ died for us."

4. *Believe and receive Christ.*
In order to have a relationship with God and an eternal home in Heaven, we must stop trusting ourselves, our works, and our religions, and place our full trust in Jesus Christ alone for the forgiveness of our sin and eternal life. Roman 10:13 says, "For everyone who calls upon the name of the Lord will be saved." That is a promise directly from God that if you will

pray to Him, confess that you are a sinner, ask Him to forgive your sins, and turn to Him alone to be your Savior, He promises to save you and give you the free gift of eternal life. You can make that decision by praying to Him today.

There are no magic words and no magic prayers. God simply desires to hear you express an understanding of your need for Him and your desire to have a relationship with Him. My prayer is that if you have not yet entered into that relationship, today is the day you accept His gift of salvation and begin living in relationship with your Creator.

About The Authors

Chad M. Robichaux, BCPC, MBA

Chad M. Robichaux is the president and founder of Mighty Oaks Foundation, a leading military nonprofit serving the US military active-duty and veteran communities with highly successful peer-to- peer, faith-based, combat-trauma programs and combat-resiliency conferences. Chad and his team are dedicated to helping America's military warriors and their families suffering from the unseen wounds of combat such as Post Traumatic Stress Disorder (PTSD). Their effort is on the front line to intercede and end the twenty-plus per day veteran suicide rate and the tragic divorce epidemic in military families. To date the program has more than fifteen-hundred alumni and has reached tens of thousands of active-duty service members through resiliency conferences.

Chad is a former Force Reconnaissance Marine and DoD Contractor with eight deployments to Afghanistan as part of a Joint Special Operations Command (JSOC) Task Force. He has earned an MBA from New York Institute of Technology (NYIT) and is a board- certified pastoral counselor with a focus on PTSD. Chad and his wife, Kathy, have been married for twenty-two years and have three children. After years of deployments, their family personally faced the challenges of PTSD. Through the struggles that warriors face returning home, they now share a story of a victory in Christ and have dedicated their lives to sharing that story to mentor others like them. Chad is a widely sought-after public speaker and subject matter expert on PTSD, and military and veteran issues, providing advice to the nation's highest-ranking flag officers. He has advised the current presidential administration on the best and most-effective faith-based solutions for veterans' care. Chad has testified in Veteran Courts regarding combat trauma and PTSD, has written a bestselling book on the subject, and has been featured on such media outlets as Fox News, Forbes, The O'Reilly Factor, The Blaze with Glenn Beck, USA Today, Christian Post, Focus on the Family, The 700 Club, and a short biography film by *I Am Second*.

In addition to Chad's military service, he has served our nation as a Special Agent with the US Federal Air Marshal Service and the US State Department as a Surveillance Detection Senior Program Manager. Chad is a Medal of Valor recipient for his bravery beyond the call of duty in law enforcement. Outside of his work with veterans, Chad is a third-degree Brazilian jiu-jitsu black belt and former Pro MMA World Champion who has used his platform to advocate support for America's Warriors while competing in the sport's biggest events such as NBC's World Series

of Fighting, StrikeForce, Bellator FC, and Legacy
FC.

Jeremy M. Stalnecker

Jeremy Stalnecker is the Executive Director of the Mighty Oaks Foundation. The Mighty Oaks Foundation is dedicated to helping America's military warriors and their families who are suffering from the unseen wounds of combat such as Post Traumatic Stress.

While growing up in San Jacinto, CA, Jeremy's only goal in life was to leave home and join the Marine Corps. This dream was finally realized with an active duty commission in 1999. Following Infantry Officer Course in Quantico, VA, Jeremy was assigned to First Battalion, Fifth Marines, First Marine Division as an infantry platoon commander. Serving first as a rifle platoon commander in a helicopter company and then as the platoon commander of the counter-mechanized platoon, Jeremy learned valuable leadership and communication skills that he continues to use today. In January 2003, Fifth Marines, as a part of the First Marine Division, deployed to Kuwait in support of what would become Operation Iraqi Freedom. As the war began, First Battalion, Fifth Marines was the infantry battalion used to breech the berm separating Kuwait and Iraq and secured the first major objective of the war. This led to a road march that ended with the battalion occupying Baghdad and seizing the presidential palace in northern Baghdad on the Tigris River. Throughout this movement, Jeremy and the counter-mechanized platoon provided navigation and lead security for the battalion.

While in the Marine Corps, God was working in Jeremy's life to turn his heart toward full-time ministry. Just one month after returning from Iraq, Jeremy became a staff member of his home church at Coastline Baptist in Oceanside,

CA. Here he gained ministry experience that would equip him for the further leading of God. In his role as an Assistant Pastor, he counseled and mentored many couples and individuals while also maintaining other church responsibilities. It was a great privilege for him to be able to serve in this capacity so close to Camp Pendleton since most of the people he worked with were either Marines or the family members of Marines.

In 2008, Jeremy and his family took on a new responsibility when he became the Senior Pastor, just east of San Francisco Bay at Bay Area Baptist Church in Fremont, CA. In this capacity, he continued to minister to families and individuals in a wide range of areas. After serving in the role of senior pastor for nearly seven years, the door leading to a full-time position with the Mighty Oaks Foundation opened. This move brought together both his ministry experience and military background in a way that allows him to serve and minister to many hurting veterans, service members and their families. Along with his wife Susanne and their four children, Jeremy works to reach the hurting and provide the healing found in Christ.

The Mighty Oaks Journey

When Chad Robichaux realized that countless other combat veterans face the same psychological, emotional, and spiritual challenges he did after his service in Afghanistan (challenges causing some twenty-plus suicides a day and staggering divorce rates among military families), Chad wondered to himself, Why doesn't someone do something about this? He eventually realized that the answer was, Why not me? And so began Mighty Oaks.

It is a story of God's transformational power to turn tragedy into triumph. It is a journey starting with one man's brokenness from war, one woman's willingness to fight for her family, and their faith in God's promise from Isaiah 61:3 that we can rise from the ashes and become mighty oaks of righteousness.

Many great men stepped in to mentor Chad and Kathy past their struggles, but none more than Steve Toth and Pastor Jeff Wells of WoodsEdge Community Church. It was through this church that Chad and Kathy were later ordained and commissioned as ministers and sent to begin the Mighty Oaks ministry to America's military warriors and families.

The first programs for men were launched in Westcliffe, Colorado, with non-active duty veterans. Chad and Kathy served alongside the Dave Roever Foundation for more than a year while developing the methodology that would become Mighty Oaks Warrior Programs (MOWP).

MOWP uses a grassroots approach,

empowering veterans to begin their healing and then be a positive impact on those around them. Those warriors, challenged by this peer-to-peer model, rose to meet the challenge and found hope and purpose beyond their military service, grabbing hold of a future worth living again. As they left the programs, they sent their brothers, which made the program grow rapidly, especially with warriors coming from US Marine Corps Wounded Warrior Battalion West, which housed a large population of Marine Corps combat veterans.

During this time of growth and increasing demand, Dave Roever introduced Chad to Wayne Hughes Jr. to explore the possibility of taking Mighty Oaks to El Paso de Robles, California (Interestingly, El Paso de Robles translates to "The Path of the Oaks"). We at Mighty Oaks say this was definitely a God wink! Wayne, a very successful businessman, had previously launched Serving California, a nonprofit philanthropy arm for his many companies.

It was in Wayne's heart to see the Lord's

hand over our returning American warriors, and he wanted to run a veterans' program at his ranch. He allowed MOWP to do so on the condition that if he liked the program, he'd build a lodge there to host it. He did like it, especially its results. From there a partnership between Mighty Oaks and Serving California took root, and SkyRose Lodge was built. This became the primary home of Mighty Oaks Warrior Programs. However, the rapidly increasing influx of warriors and military families has resulted in three other regional locations: Blaylock Ranch in Junction, Texas; Warrior Retreat at Bull Run in Haymarket, Virginia; and The Wilds in Columbus, Ohio.

As our work continues with veterans and spouses, we receive active-duty warriors on official orders from the various branches. We also have become a top resource for the US military, having trained and equipped more than one hundred thousand warriors in combat readiness through Resiliency Conferences at bases across the country. This included Chad and Jeremy authoring The Path to Resiliency, a spiritual-resiliency book used as a resource for the US military.

Even though Mighty Oaks Warrior Programs has expanded in both numbers and geographic locations, our vision remains the same: to assist our nation's warriors and families by challenging, equipping, and empowering them to take the help they receive and spread it to those in their own circles of influence. We now have more than fifteen-hundred Mighty Oaks alumni, and we take great pride in not having lost one to suicide to date. Beyond each warrior's healing they are challenged, equipped, and empowered to care for his brothers, bringing both a solution to the problem and a purpose for those willing to share that solution with others.

Together, we can all strive toward the common goal of ending the war at home by finding a hope and a future, and aligning with the purpose for which God created us. We will continue to lead others to fulfill the promise of Isaiah 61:3: to rise from the ashes and become mighty oaks!

Fully paid scholarships are available for all MOWP for active-duty or veteran military personnel, as well as their spouses, by applying online. For more information on programs, or on how you can participate in donating or supporting MOWP, visit:

www.MightyOaksPrograms.org

References

1. PTSd.va.gov/professional

2. Trimble, M.D. (1985). Post-traumatic
    Stress Disorder: History of a concept. In
    C.R. Figley (Ed.), Trauma and its wake:
    The study and treatment of Post-Traumatic
    Stress Disorder. New York: Brunner/
    Mazel. Revised from Encyclopedia of
    Psychology, R. Corsini, Ed. (New York:
    Wiley, 1984, 1994)

3. Diagnostic and Statistical Manual of
    Mental Disorders, Fifth Edition,2013 pp.
    271

4. Sethanne Howard and Mark W. Crandall,
    MD, Post Traumatic Stress Disorder-
    What happens in the Brain?, Washington
    Academy of Sciences, Fall 2007

5. www.valuesbasedmanagement.net/
methods_boyd_ooda_loop.html

6. www.learning-theories.com/operant-
conditioning-skinner.html

7. www.PTSd.va.gov

8. Diagnostic and Statistical Manual of
Mental Disorders, Fifth Edition,2013 pp.
265

9. Viktor Frankl, Man' Search for Meaning,
Beacon Press, 1959

10. Ibid.

11. Ibid.

MIGHTY OAKS WARRIOR PROGRAMS

LEGACY PROGRAM FOR MEN - Our six-day intensive peer to peer program serves as the catalyst to help Warriors discover the answers to the big questions in life. Challenges related to the struggles of daily military life, combat deployments and the symptoms of post-traumatic stress (PTS) surface during these six days, and the Legacy Program for Men teaches how to fight through these challenges, which might have been limiting their personal success.

LEGACY PROGRAM FOR WOMEN - The Legacy Program for Women is a process of learning to become a Virtuous Woman – "The Proverbs 31" woman. This three-day retreat leads spouses and military women through a time of learning, exploration and growth with an aim to cultivate virtuous characteristics in a safe, open, nurturing environment.

MARRIAGE ADVANCE: LOVE NEVER GIVES UP - Our three day Marriage Advance Program is designed for couples to gain a better understanding of the struggles they each face. We structure conversations around needs, expectations, goals and forgiveness to help couples move forward.

MILITARY RESILIENCY PROGRAMS - We believe that *"Resiliency"* is comprised of three pillars: *mind, body and spirit.* Our Military Resiliency Programs are designed to properly equip our nation's Warriors on the front end of conflict, so they and their families can have a true *"Resiliency"* and a mindset that is preventative of the hardships that many of them face.

These programs are NO cost to our Warriors.
To support or learn more please visit:

www.MightyOaksPrograms.org

An official program of Mighty Oaks Foundation, a 501c3 Non-Profit Organization

The Mighty Oaks Speaker's Team

Will deliver powerful presentations to various audiences including:

✪ **CORPORATE OUTINGS**

✪ **CHURCH SERVICES & EVENTS**

✪ **MILITARY EVENTS**

✪ **RESILIENCY CONFERENCES**

✪ **MEN'S EVENTS**

Our speakers are combat Veterans, or spouses of combat Veterans and have a passion to share the transformational experience that changed their world and unveiled their purpose.

Our presentations on the following topics are both inspiring and challenging and can be scaled from single sessions to multi-day/multi-session retreats and conferences.

✪ **LEADERSHIP**

✪ **LIVING A PURPOSEFUL LIFE**

✪ **FORGIVENESS**

✪ **CHARACTER**

✪ **LEGACY**

✪ **MANHOOD**

✪ **MARRIAGE**

Contact us at:
MightyOaksPrograms.org/Speakers

OTHER MIGHTY OAKS RESOURCES

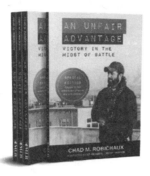

✪ An Unfair Advantage ✪
By Chad Robichaux

Take a journey with Force Recon Marine and Pro Mixed Martial Arts Champion Fighter, Chad Robichaux, as he shares a glimpse into the life of special operations, competition as a professional fighter, and the deep insight into this world's spiritual battles which we are all engaged. Chad shares personal stories of both success and failure experienced in Afghanistan, the MMA cage, and his biggest fight of all... coming home and facing a struggle with PTSD, a near divorce and almost becoming another veteran suicide statistic. Each chapter shares a parallel story of Biblical-time warriors who faced similar struggles and reveals *An Unfair Advantage* that led them to victory in the midst of those battles. Discover that same advantage for the battles you face and unlock the warrior spirit sewn in your heart by God Himself.

✪ Path to Resiliency ✪
By Chad Robichaux & Jeremy Stalnecker

This book was written to challenge the greatest of Warriors, whether military or civilian, man or woman... to be ready for, resilient to, and able to reintegrate from life's trials and rigors. You don't have to go to Iraq or Afghanistan to face the hardships and trials of life! Military service member or not, we all find ourselves in moments of adversity and hardship from time to time. When we do, will you have the resiliency to overcome.

As I work with those suffering from combat trauma, PTS and a deep hopelessness, I have witnessed miraculous redemption. The lie that these Warriors have "no tomorrow" dissipates, when they turn to God to find hope in their darkest hours. I have seen what the prophet Ezekiel witnessed in the valley of dry bones. I've seen dry bones come to life.

– Chad M. Robichaux,
Founder of Mighty Oaks Foundation